There are several Eva Cassidy songbooks on the market, but this one was created especially for guitar and voice. Each guitar arrangement in this book has been transcribed from the Eva Cassidy CDs. Eva left us no musical notation or even sheet music from which she learned. In addition, we have added some of Eva's drawings to create a very personalized songbook.

The guitar was Eva's constant companion from an early age. I first taught her guitar chords when she was barely nine years old. I was at that time working as a bass player in order to supplement the family income.

Once Eva perfected her guitar chords, she was anxious to play her favourite folk and jazz tunes. Eva probably spent a great deal more time in her room teaching herself guitar techniques than she spent on her homework. Eva spent countless hours absorbing the unique talents of artists in her own eclectic record collection and then she worked out her own arrangements in her head.

In high school, and later at community college, Eva sang and played with various groups including Stonehenge and Excalliber. She also performed as a soloist, singing her wonderful arrangements and accompanying herself on guitar.

When we were approached initially about Eva songbooks, I immediately thought that there should be a book specifically designed for guitar players. We were fortunate in finding Christina Davidson and we were able to work closely with her in creating this book. Christina is a music copyist and calligrapher with years of experience creating music for various publications. She also turned out to be a big fan of Eva's work. This guitar songbook is a testament to Christina Davidson's talents and also her appreciation for Eva's style and arrangements.

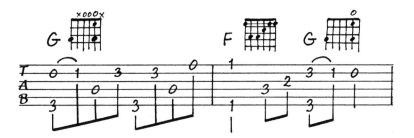

The guitar arrangements are very simple and playable. Eva used basic first-position chords and Christina has provided instruction as to where the capo should be placed in order to play each song, in key, along with Eva on her CDs.

Eva loved suspensions and employed a finger-picking style which is very pleasing. You will experience her simple, yet effective arpeggios and folk patterns when you work with the tablature portion of each song. Make sure that you read the glossary at the end of the book for an explanation of the tablature and other notes from Christina.

Eva would have liked the look of the hand-copied music – she was a very gifted artist as well as a musician. The illustrations in this book were all done by Eva and include many of her whimsical sketches, caricatures and beautiful pictures.

The selection of songs
was carefully considered. . . .

Of course, we wanted to include
Over the Rainbow as first heard on
"The Other Side" and released in 1992.
This now famous arrangement by Eva is
also on the later CD entitled "Songbird."

Fields of Gold was recorded in 1996 on
Eva's first solo record entitled "Live at
Blues Alley." It was also later released on
"Songbird." Eva's version of this song is
the one of the most requested tunes for
compilation albums.

Eva grew up in the 60s and 70s. As a
youngster, her mother and I were playing
LP's by Pete Seeger, Buffy St. Marie and
Ray Charles, just to name a few. I was
working with Eva and her brother Dan and
sisters Anette and Margaret to create
a family group to perform at holiday and
family functions. During this period of
time, Eva gained appreciation and love for
spirituals and folk melodies such as
Wade in the Water, Do Lord (retitled
Way Beyond the Blue) and
Wayfaring Stranger.

At the time Eva's illness was diagnosed,
she was planning a solo tour of Eastern
Canada, Iceland and Europe and I know that
her repertoire included these selections.

The Cassidy family record collection also included LPs by Louis Armstrong, Ella Fitzgerald and Aretha Franklin. Many people have remarked at Eva's wide-ranging selection of material, but I know exactly which artists and which LPs piqued her interest. From this genre of music, we include: What a Wonderful World, Autumn Leaves and At Last.

Eva had an attraction to several tunes written by Christine McVie. Songbird, the tune, is included in this book and the arrangement is absolutely true to Eva's recording of it.

I personally like the tenderness and message of Steve Digman's Anniversary Song. Steve hired Eva to do a demonstration recording of his original material, and we were most delighted, after Eva's passing, when we heard that this tune would be made available for Eva's CD entitled "Time After Time."

I have always felt that the simplicity of guitar and voice is one of God's many gifts. Whether one plays guitar at home, alone, for the sheer joy of making music -- or whether you join with others around a campfire or at family gatherings, it's food for the soul. I hope that this book of Eva's special material will become dog-eared over the years, as you too enjoy the wondrous experience of "making music."

Best regards,
Hugh Cassidy

The Eva Cassidy
SONGBOOK for GUITAR

Ain't No Sunshine 17
Anniversary Song 14
At Last 10
Autumn Leaves 6
Fields of Gold 36
I Wandered by a Brookside 21
Nightbird 40
Over the Rainbow 27
Penny to My Name 44
Say Goodbye 48
Songbird 51
Time After Time 55
Wade in the Water 63
Way Beyond the Blue 66
Wayfaring Stranger 33
What a Wonderful World 59

All artwork is by Eva Cassidy
Photos are from the Cassidy Family & friends
Music & verses are hand-lettered by
Christina Davidson

Autumn Leaves

as sung by Eva Cassidy

The falling leaves drift by my window, the falling leaves of red and gold.
I see your lips, the summer kisses, the sunburned hands I used to hold.

Since you went away the days grow long, and soon I'll hear old winter's song.
But I miss you most of all, my darling, when autumn leaves start to fall.

Since you went away the days grow long,
and soon I'll hear old winter's song.
But I miss you most of all, my darling,
when autumn leaves start to fall.

I miss you most of all, my darling,
when autumn leaves start to fall.

Autumn Leaves

Words by Jacques Prevert
Music by Joseph Kosma
English Translation by Johnny Mercer

Slowly, with expression
[Capo 1st fret]

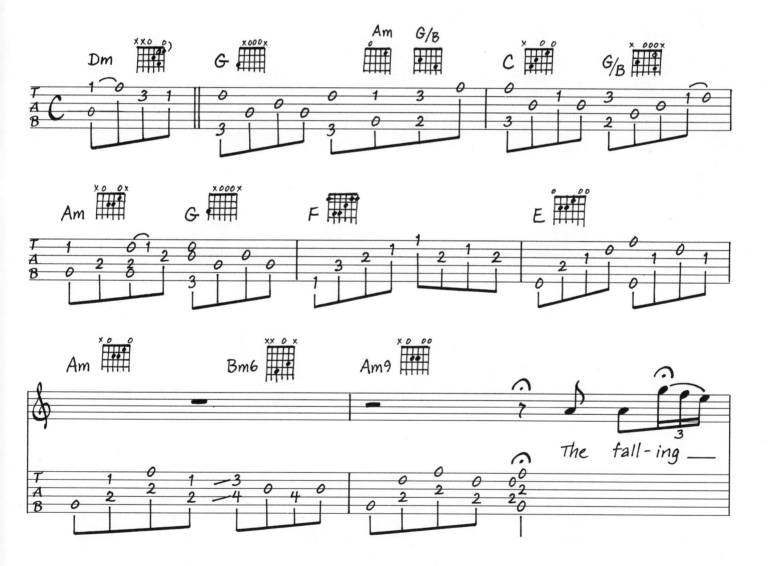

The fall-ing ___

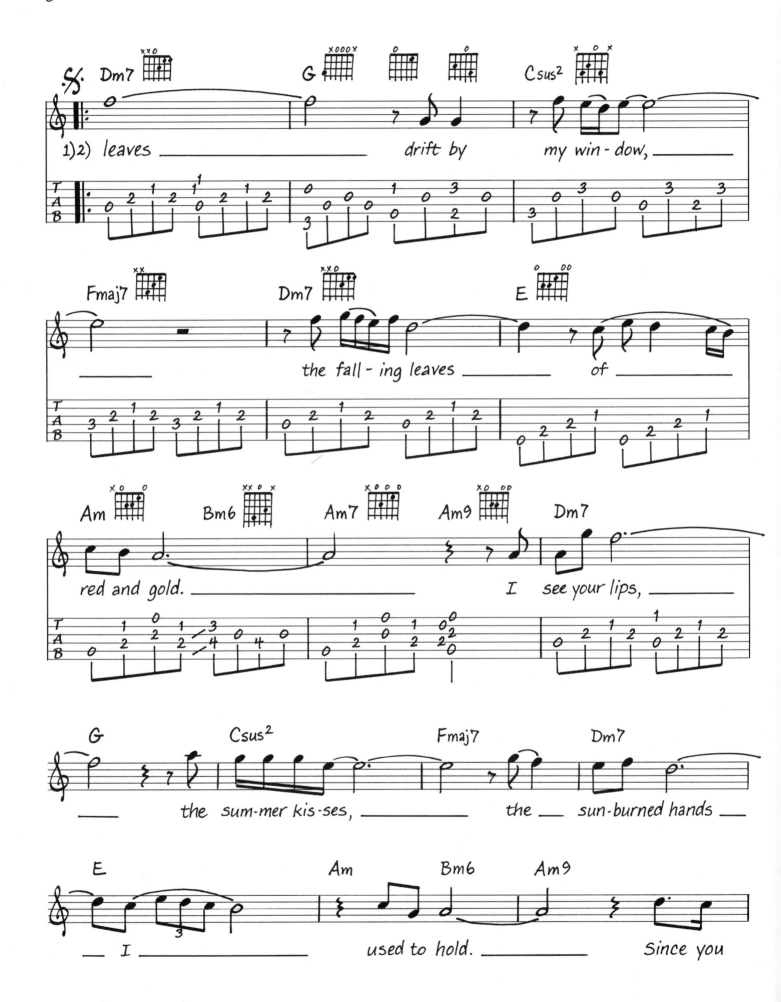

At Last
as sung by Eva Cassidy

At last, my love has come along,
my lonely days are over
and life is like a song.
Oh, yeah.

At last, the skies above are blue,
and my heart was wrapped in clover
the night I looked at you.

I found a dream that I could speak to,
a dream that I could call my own.
I found a thrill to press my cheek to,
a thrill that I have never known,
oh, yeah.

You smiled, oh, and then the spell was cast,
and here we are in heaven
for you are mine at last,
for you are mine at last.

At Last

Slow blues, in 2

[Open - no capo]

Words by Mack Gordon,
Music by Harry Warren

At last, _____

my ___ love ___ has come a - long, _____

my lone - ly days ___ are o - ver _____

and life is like ___ a song. _____ Oh ___

12

Anniversary Song

as sung by Eva Cassidy

Today has been a special day, an anniversary, a request,
that you play your piano as the evening sun slowly sets.
I never thought I'd get this old dear, never had a reason to live so long,
and the Lord's been like my shadow, even when I was wrong.
No, I never thought it would turn out this way.

A birthday with apologies for all the tears and regrets,
and I've always saved your poetry for these years when you forget.
I never thought I'd get this old dear, never had a reason to live so long,
and the Lord's been like my shadow, even when I was wrong.
No, I never thought it would turn out this way.

So sing with me softly as the day turns to night,
and later I'll dream of paradise with you.
I love you and goodnight.

Anniversary Song

Words & Music by Steven Digman

Slowly & gently
[Open – no capo]

Ain't No Sunshine

as sung by Eva Cassidy

Ain't no sunshine when he's gone,
it's not warm when he's away.
Ain't no sunshine when he's gone,
and he's always gone too long
anytime he goes away.

I wonder this time where he's gone,
wonder how long he's gonna stay.
Ain't no sunshine when he's gone,
and this house just ain't no home
anytime he goes away.

Well, I know, I know, I know, I know,
I know, I know, I know, I know, I know,
I know, I know, I know, I know, I know,
I know, I know, I know, I know, when he's gone,
always gone too long
anytime he goes away,
anytime he goes away,
anytime he goes.

Ain't No Sunshine

Moderate Blues

Words & Music by Bill Withers

[Open – no capo]
This arrangement does not include the guitar solos
played by Eva's band members.

Ain't no sun-shine __ when he's gone, ___

it's not warm__ when ___ he's __ a-way. ___

I Wandered by a Brookside

as sung by Eva Cassidy

I wandered by a brookside, I wandered by a mill.
I could not hear the water, the murmuring it was still.
Not a sound of any grasshopper nor the chirp of any bird.
But the beating of my own heart, was the only sound I heard.
The beating of my own heart, was the only sound I heard.

Then silent tears fast growing, when someone stood beside.
A hand upon my shoulder, I knew the touch was kind.
He drew me near the mirror, we neither spoke one word.
But the beating of our own two hearts, was the only sound I heard.
The beating of our own two hearts, was the only sound I heard.

I Wandered By A Brookside

Words Traditional, Music by Barbara Berry

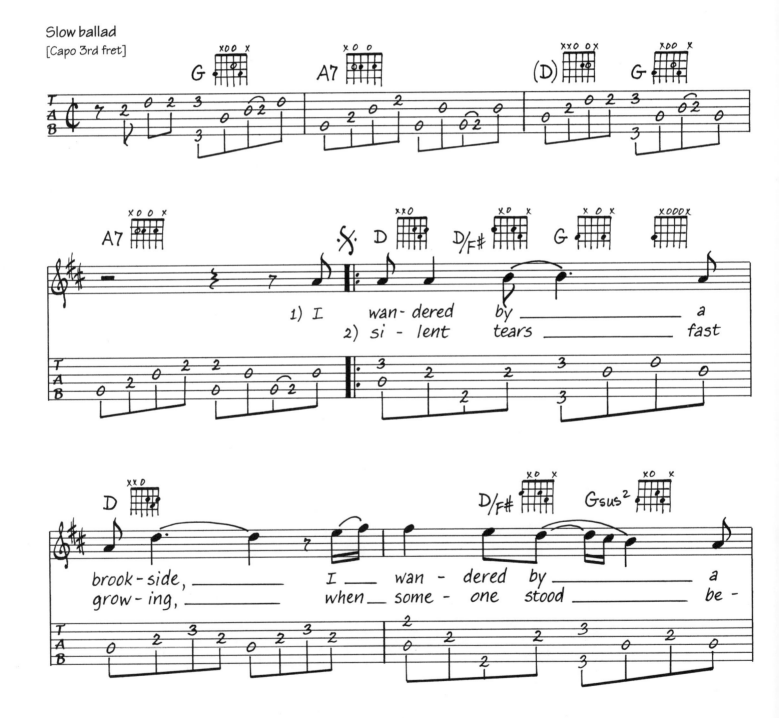

24

Over the Rainbow

as sung by Eva Cassidy

Somewhere over the rainbow way up high,
in a land that I heard of once,
once in a lullaby.

Somewhere over the rainbow skies are blue,
and the dreams that you dared to dream
really do come true.

Someday I'll wish upon a star
and wake up where the clouds are far behind me.
Where troubles melt like lemon drops
away above the chimney tops,
that's where you'll find me.

Somewhere over the rainbow skies are blue,
and the dreams that you dared to dream
really do come true.

If happy little bluebirds fly
above the rainbow,
why, oh why can't I?

Over the Rainbow

Words by E. Y. Harburg, Music by Harold Arlen

Slowly & Freely

[Capo 1st fret]

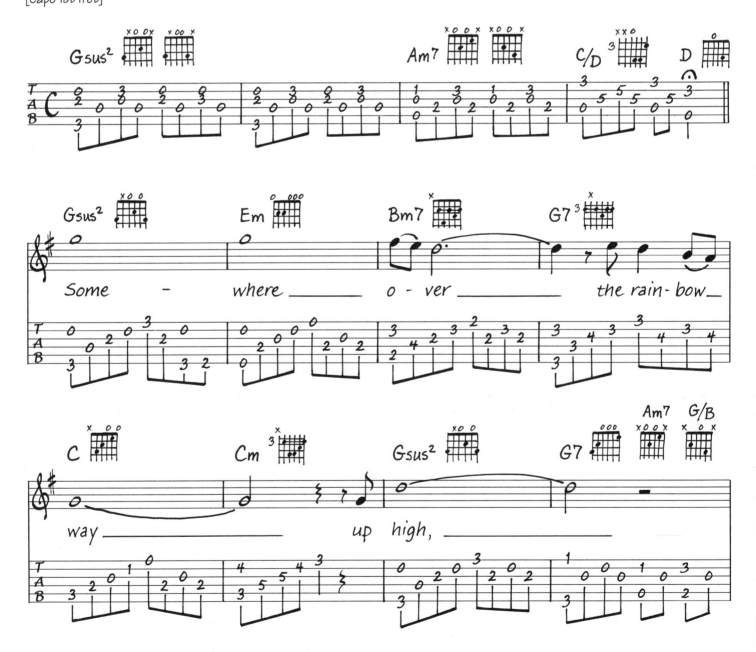

Some — where _____ o - ver _____ the rain- bow__

way _____ up high, _____

Some - day ___ I'll wish up-on a star___ and wake up where the

clouds are far ___ be - hind ___ me. ___ where ___

___ trou - bles ___ melt like le-mon drops a-way a-bove

the chim-ney tops, that's where ___ you'll ___ find ___ me. ___

Wayfaring Stranger

as sung by Eva Cassidy

I am a poor wayfaring stranger, while journeying through this world of woe.
Yet there's no sickness toil or danger in that bright land to which I go.
I'm going there to see my father, I'm going there no more to roam.
I'm only going over Jordan, I'm only going over home.

I know dark clouds will gather o'er me, I know my way is rough and steep.
Yet beautiful fields lie just before me that God's redeeming vigils keep.
I'm going there to see my mother, I'm going there no more to roam.
I'm only going over Jordan, I'm only going over home.

I'm going there to see my mother, I'm going there no more to roam.
I'm only going over Jordan, I'm only going over home.

I want to wear that crown of glory, when I get home to that good land.
I want to shout salvation's story in concert with the blood-washed band.
I'm going there to see my Savior, I'm going there no more to roam.
I'm only going over Jordan, I'm only going over home.

I'm only going over Jordan, I'm only going over home.

Wayfaring Stranger

Traditional
Arranged by Eva Cassidy

Moderate Folk (or Blues, ad lib)

[Capo 1st fret]

This arrangement is Eva's folk version that she played as a soloist.

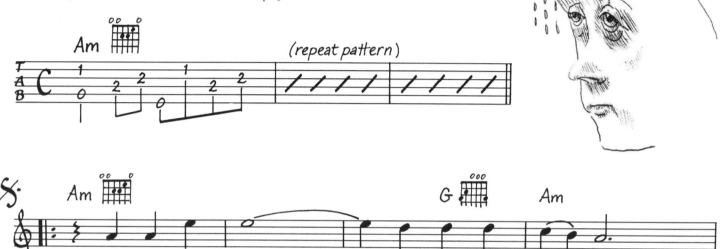

1) I am a poor _____ way-far-ing stran-ger, _____
2) I know dark clouds _____ will ga-ther o'er me, _____
3) I want to wear _____ that crown of glo-ry, _____

while jour-ney-ing through _____ this world of woe. _____
I know _ my way _____ is rough and steep. _____
when I _ get home _____ to that good land. _____

yet there's no sick — ness, toil or dan-ger _____
yet beauti-ful fields _____ lie just be-fore me _____
I want to shout _____ sal-va-tion's sto-ry _____

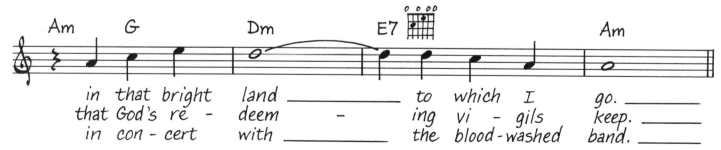

in that bright land _____ to which I go. _____
that God's re-deem — ing vi-gils keep. _____
in con-cert with _____ the blood-washed band. _____

Fields of Gold

as sung by Eva Cassidy

Ooh, you'll remember me when the west wind moves among the fields of barley.
You can tell the sun in his jealous sky when we walked in fields of gold.

So she took her love for to gaze awhile among the fields of barley.
In his arms she fell as her hair came down among the fields of gold.
Will you stay with me, will you be my love among the fields of barley?
And you can tell the sun in his jealous sky when we walked in fields of gold.

I never made promises lightly and there have been some that I've broken.
But I swear in the days still left we will walk in fields of gold,
We'll walk in fields of gold.

Many years have passed since those summer days among the fields of barley.
See the children run as the sun goes down as you lie in fields of gold.
You'll remember me when the west wind moves among the fields of barley.
You can tell the sun in his jealous sky when we walked in fields of gold.
When we walked in fields of gold,
when we walked in fields of gold.

Fields of Gold

Moderate ballad

[Capo 7th fret]

Words & Music by Gordon Sumner

© 1993 Steerpike Ltd
Magnetic Publishing Ltd, London WC2H OQY

Nightbird

as sung by Eva Cassidy

Some old hotel room in Memphis, I see the city through the rain.
I'm just chasing me my time and remembering some pain.
You see there once was a boy, and on the streets he'd surely die.
So the nightbird took him in, and she taught him how to fly.
See the nightbird softly fly. Why does she fly alone?
Is the moonlight just a flame for her memory? Now she's gone.

Two bit bars and honkytonks, any pleasure can be found.
You can get just what you want if you lay your money down.
And lonely sailors do their drinking, my, my, my, how the brave men do die.
And the nightbird sells her pleasures, bringing tears to my eyes.
See the nightbird softly fly. Why does she fly alone?
Is the moonlight just a flame for her memory? Now she's gone.

So I guess I'll go out walking, Lord, let the rain keep fallin' down.
I guess I'll go and chase some memories, in the dark side of town.
See the nightbird softly fly. Why does she fly alone?
Is the moonlight just a flame for her memory? Now she's gone,
For her memory? Now she's gone.
For her memory? Now she's gone.

Nightbird

Words & Music by Douglas MacLeod

Moderate Country ballad
[Open – no capo]

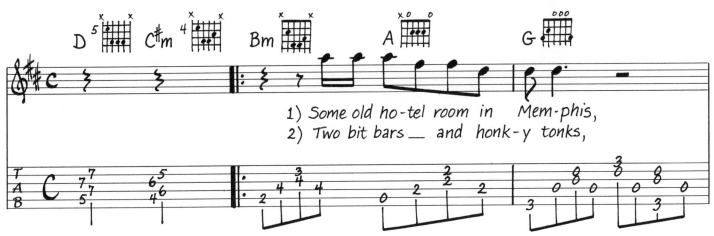

1) Some old ho-tel room in Mem-phis,
2) Two bit bars and honk-y tonks,

I see the cit-y through the rain. _____ I'm just chas - ing
an-y plea-sure can _____ be found. _____ You can get just

me my_ time _____ and re-mem-ber-ing some_ pain. _____
what you_ want _____ if you lay_ your mon - ey _____ down. _____

42

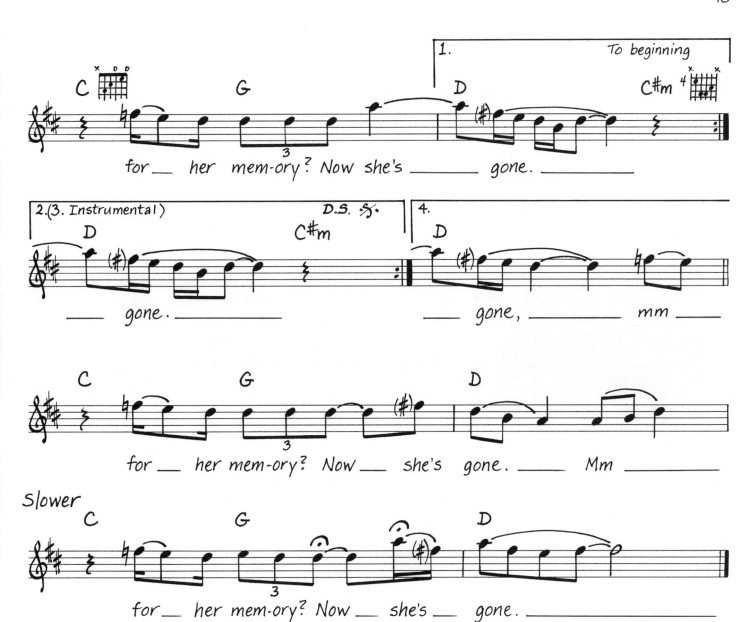

for __ her mem-ory? Now she's _____ gone. _____

gone. _____ __ gone, _____ mm ___

for __ her mem-ory? Now __ she's gone. ___ Mm _____

Slower

for __ her mem-ory? Now __ she's __ gone. _____

Penny To My Name

as sung by Eva Cassidy

Bill and I got married following our firstborn,
Daddy left his gas and convenience store just before he died.
And I was only nineteen when I had my third baby.
Sometimes I think maybe I should have left here long ago.

Travelers are stoppin' by, check their oil and their P.S.I.
Gas up and away they fly, movin' down the line.
But this beat-up truck and worn out shoes,
always givin' me the blues.
Billy suckin' down the booze, nearly ev'ry night.

I've never seen the city lights, how they must shine so bright.
Not unlike this country night, the sky's black as coal.
And this gas station mountain home, not a thing to call my own.
How I wish I was alone with a penny to my name.

Strangers see this mountain here is beautiful beyond compare,
but it's just a dumb old mountain there, I see it ev'ry day.
If I could see a sunset sky, over fields of grain or ocean tides.
City skyline in the night, I'll be dancin' 'til the dawn.

I've never seen the city lights, how they must shine so bright.
Not unlike this country night, the sky's black as coal.
And this gas station mountain home, not a thing to call my own.
How I wish I was alone with a penny to my name.

Bill and I got married following our firstborn,
Daddy left his gas and convenience store just before he died.
Maybe Bill and I someday will find a chance to get away.
Until then it's here I'll stay, wishin' on a star.

I've never seen the city lights, how they must shine so bright.
Not unlike this country night, the sky's black as coal.
And this gas station mountain home, not a thing to call my own.
How I wish I was alone with a penny to my name, penny to my name.

Penny To My Name

Moderate Country

Words & Music by Roger Henderson

[Open – no capo]

may-be I __ should have left _____ here long__ a - go. _____

VERSE:

C   Fmaj7

1) Trav - elers   are stop-pin' by, _____   check their oil   and their
2) Stran-gers see this moun-tain here   is   beau - ti - ful ____ be -
3) Bill and I got mar-ried _____   fol - low-ing ___ our

Fmaj7   Dm

P. S.   I. _____   Gas up and   a - way__ they fly, ____
yond com - pare, ___ but it's   just a dumb old   moun - tain there, ___
first-born, _____ Dad-dy   left his gas and con -venience store _____

G   C

mov-in' down   the line. _____ But this   beat - up truck and
(I) see it ev - 'ry day. _____ If   I could see   a
just be-fore   he died. _____   May-be Bill   and

C   Fmaj7

worn out shoes, _____ al - ways ____ giv-in' me   the blues. ____
sun-set sky, __ o-ver fields of grain ____ or   o - cean tides. ____
I some-day __ will __ find a   chance to ___ get a - way. ____

Dm   G

Bill-y suck-in' ___ down__the booze,   near-ly ev - 'ry   night. ____
Cit-y sky-line ___ in __ the night,   I'll be danc-in' 'til the dawn. ____
Un-til then it's ___ here I'll stay, _____ wish-in' on a   star. ____

CHORUS:

I've nev-er seen the cit-y lights, how they must shine so bright. ___

Not un-like ___ this coun-try night, ___ the sky's ___ black as

coal. _____ And this gas sta - tion moun-tain ___ home, _____

not a thing ___ to call my own. _____ How I wish ___ I

was a-lone ___ with a pen-ny ___ to my name. _____

pen·ny to ___ my name. _____

pen - ny _____ to _____ my name. _____

Say Goodbye

as sung by Eva Cassidy

It's funny how the distance can make you feel close,
of the things you lost are the things you want most.
The weather's fine here, a perfect shade of blue.
I guess that's why I've been thinking of you.

So I'll call you up just to tell you why, why I left you and said goodbye.
Oh it must be the mood I'm in, I'm thinking of you again.
I call you up just to tell you why, why I left you and said goodbye.

I know you're different now and I guess I've changed too,
and I thought what once was right, was so wrong for you.
Yesterday I was talking and I heard your name.
The weather's fine here, with a slight chance of rain.

So I'll call you up just to tell you why, why I left you and said goodbye.
Oh it must be the mood I'm in, I'm thinking of you again.
I call you up just to tell you why, why I left you and said goodbye.

Time makes you sorry for the things that you've done.
Sometimes you walk away and sometimes you run.
The weather's fine here, I can feel a slight chill.
Some things change babe, and some never will.

So I'll call you up just to tell you why, why I left you and said goodbye.
Oh it must be the mood I'm in, I'm thinking of you again.
I call you up just to tell you why, why I left you and said goodbye.

I call you up just to tell you why, why I left you and said goodbye.
I call you up just to tell you why, to say I love you and to say goodbye.

Say Goodbye

Moderate, in 2
[Open - no capo]

Words & Music by
Steven Digman & Andrew Hernandez

VERSE:

1) It's fun-ny how the dis-tance can make you feel __ close, __
2) I know you're different now __ and I guess I've changed too, __
3) __ Time makes you sor-ry for the things that you've done. __

of the things you lost __ are the things you want __ most. __
and I thought what once was right, was so wrong __ for you. __
Some-times you walk a-way and some-times you __ run.

The wea-ther's fine __ here, __ a per-fect shade __ of blue.
__ yes-ter-day I was talk-ing and I heard your __ name.
The wea-ther's fine __ here, __ I can feel a slight __ chill.

I guess that's why I've been __ think-ing of you. __ So I'll
The wea-ther's fine here, with a slight chance of rain. __ So I'll
Some __ things change __ babe, and some __ never will. __ So I'll

CHORUS:

call you up __ just to tell __ you why, __

Songbird

as sung by Eva Cassidy

For you, there'll be no cryin'.
For you, the sun will be shining.
'Cause I feel that when I'm with you,
it's alright. I know it's right.
And the songbirds keep singing like they know the score.
And I love you, I love you, I love you like never before.

To you, I would give the world.
To you, I'd never be cold.
'Cause I feel that when I'm with you,
it's alright. I know it's right.
And the songbirds keep singing like they know the score.
And I love you, I love you, I love you like never before,
like never before, like never before.

Songbird

Slowly, with feeling
[Open - no capo]

Words & Music by Christine McVie

Time After Time

as sung by Eva Cassidy

Lying in my bed I hear the clock tick and think of you.
Turning in circles, confusion is nothing new.
Flashback to warm nights, almost left behind,
a suitcase of memories, time after. . .

Sometimes you picture me, I'm walking too far ahead.
You're calling to me, I can't hear what you have said.
You say, "Go slow," I've fallen behind. The second hand unwinds.
If you're lost you can look and you will find me, time after time.
If you fall I will catch you, I'll be waiting, time after time.
If you fall I will catch you, I will be waiting,
time after time, time after time.

After your picture fades and darkness has turned to grey,
watching through windows I'm wondering if you're OK
And you say "Go slow," I've fallen behind. The drum beats out of time.
If you're lost you can look and you will find me, time after time.
If you fall I will catch you, I'll be waiting, time after time.
If you fall I will catch you, I will be waiting,
time after time, time after time.
Time after time.
Oh, time after time,
time after time.

Time After Time

Moderately, with a jazz feeling

[Capo 2nd fret]

Words & Music by
Robert Hyman & Cyndi Lauper

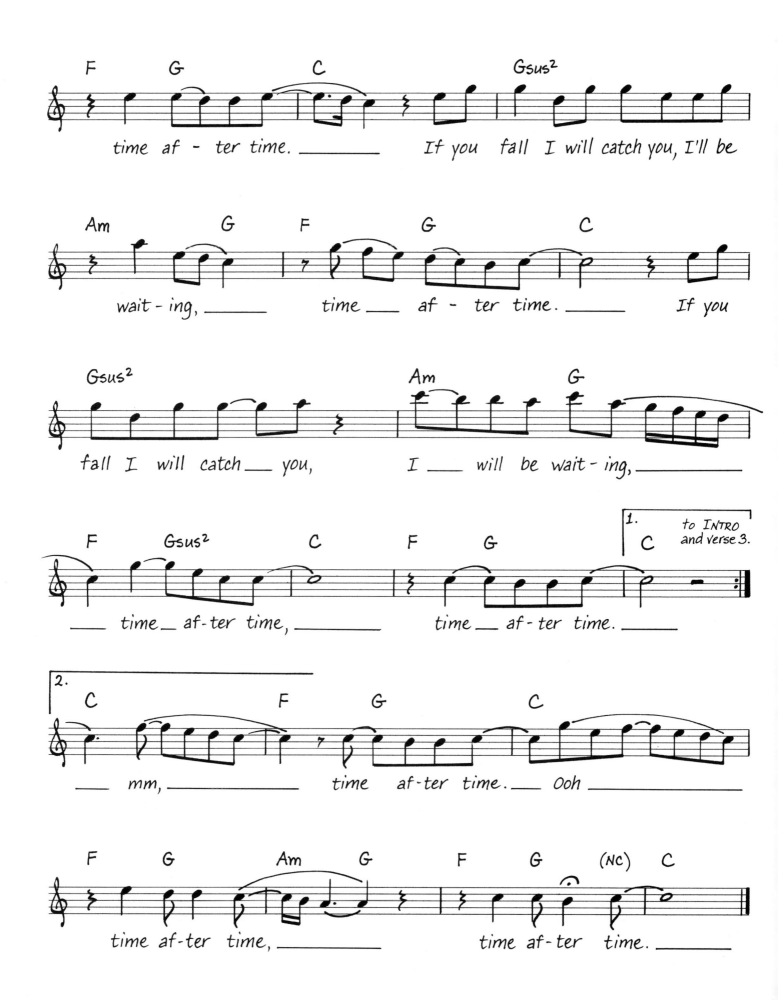

What a Wonderful World

as sung by Eva Cassidy

I see trees that are green, red roses too.
I'll watch them bloom for me and you.
And I think to myself, what a wonderful world.

I hear babies cry, I watch them grow.
And they'll learn much more than I'll ever know,
and I think to myself, Oh, what a wonderful world.

The colors of the rainbow so pretty in the sky,
are also on the faces of the people passing by.

I see friends shaking hands saying "How do you do?"
But they're really saying "I love you."

I see trees that are green, red roses too.
I'll watch them bloom for me and you.
And I think to myself, what a wonderful world.

I think to myself,
Oh, what a wonderful world.

What a Wonderful World

Words & Music by George Weiss and Bob Thiele

Slowly, in 2

[Open – no capo]

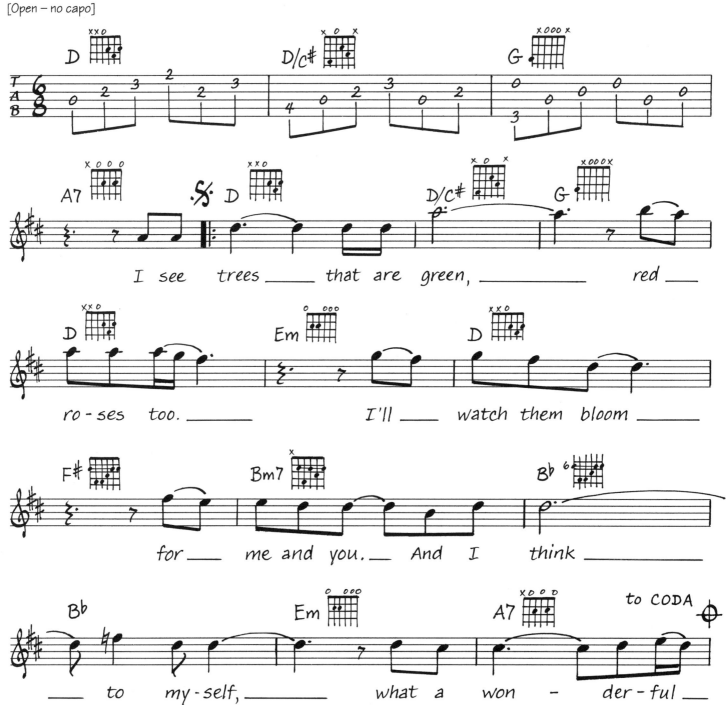

I see trees ____ that are green, _____ red ___

ro - ses too. _____ I'll ___ watch them bloom _____

for ___ me and you. ___ And I think _____

___ to my - self, ____ what a won - der - ful ___

to CODA

Wade in the Water

as sung by Eva Cassidy

Wade in the water, wade in the water children.
Wade in the water. God's gonna trouble the water.

Who's that yonder dressed in red? Wade in the water.
Must be the children that Moses led. God's gonna trouble the water.
Oh, wade in the water, wade in the water children.
Wade in the water. God's gonna trouble the water.

Who's that yonder dressed in white? Wade in the water.
Must be the children of the Israelite. God's gonna trouble the water.
Oh, wade in the water, wade in the water children.
Wade in the water. God's gonna trouble the water.

Who's that yonder dressed in blue? Wade in the water.
Must be the children that's coming through. God's gonna trouble the water.
Oh, wade in the water, wade in the water children.
Wade in the water. God's gonna trouble the water.

You don't believe I've been redeemed. Wade in the water.
Must be the Holy Ghost lookin' for me. God's gonna trouble the water.
Oh, wade in the water, wade in the water children.
Wade in the water. God's gonna trouble the water.

Wade in the Water

Traditional
Arranged by Eva Cassidy

Moderate Blues
[Capo 1st fret]

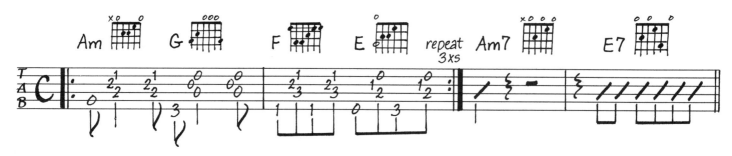

wade in the wa - ter,   wade   in   the

wa ter chil - dren.   Wade _____   in the wa-ter. _____

God's gon-na trou - ble the   wa _____ ter. _____

VERSE:

1) who's that yon - der ____ dressed in red? ____   wade ___ in the
2) who's that yon - der ____ dressed in white? ____   wade ___ in the
3) 4) who's that yon - der ____ dressed in blue? ____   wade ___ in the
5) you don't be - lieve I've been re - deemed. ____   wade ___ in the

wa - ter. ____ Must be the chil - dren that Mo - ses led. ____
wa - ter. ____ Must be the chil - dren of the Is - rae - lite. ____
wa - ter. ____ Must be the chil - dren that's com - ing through. ___
wa - ter. ____ Must be the Holy Ghost ____ look-in' for me. ____

God's gon-na trou-ble the wa - ter. Oh,   wade ____ in the

CHORUS:

wa - ter, ____   wade in the wa-ter chil - dren.   Wade _____

Last time: repeat
CHORUS and fade

in the wa - ter. ___ God's gon-na trou-ble the wa - ter. _____

(3rd verse: inst. solo)

Way Beyond the Blue

as sung by Eva Cassidy

Oh do Lord, oh do Lord, oh do you remember me?
Oh do Lord, oh do Lord, oh do you remember me?
Do Lord, oh do Lord, oh do you remember me,
way beyond the blue.

Oh I got a home in Glory Land that outshines the sun,
I've got a home in Glory Land that outshines the sun.
I got a home in Glory Land that outshines the sun,
way beyond the blue.

Oh do Lord, oh do Lord, oh do you remember me?
Oh do Lord, oh do Lord, oh do you remember me?
Oh do Lord, oh do Lord, oh do you remember me,
way beyond the blue.

Way Beyond the Blue

Gospel style, acappella
[Optional guitar: capo 2nd fret]

Traditional
Arranged by Eva Cassidy

68